IT'S ALL ABOUT
Cards & Tags

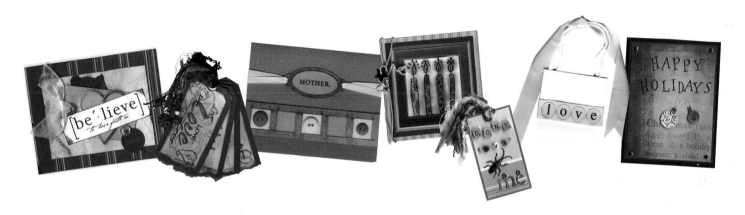

A Leisure Arts Publication by
Nancy M. Hill of

D1119471

Acknowledgments

It's All About Cards & Tags is the fifth in a series
of books written by NanC and Company and
published by Leisure Arts, Inc.

Author: Nancy M. Hill
Design Director: Candice Snyder
Senior Editor: Candice Smoot
Graphic Artist: Rafael Nielson
Photographer: Julianne Smoot
Cover Design: Maren Ogden
Copy Editor: Sharon Staples
Cover Layouts: Bea Elizalde
                    Martha Crowther
In House Designers:
                    Nancy M. Hill
                    Erin Madsen
                    Candice Smoot
                    Candice Snyder
                    Maren Ogden

For information about sales visit the
Leisure Arts web site at www.leisurearts.com.

We have had so much fun designing *It's All About Cards & Tags*! As card makers and scrapbookers how could we not enjoy the process of creating and selecting cards and tags from our exceptionally talented team of designers and submitters!

A hand made card is often a gift in itself—and most of us don't throw out a personalized card with the gift-wrap. Of all the cards and tags we could have featured on this page, we chose a card given to me by a very special neighborhood teenager with a quick wit and darling personality. It isn't the ornate quality of the paper or the use of design principles that makes me love this card; it's simply reflective of her fun personality. At 15 years old, her choice of combining a simple graphic with a grown up message is endearing. Cards such as these are treasures that become part of my "save forever" collection of memorabilia!

From simple to complex, we have chosen a variety of examples you can gather ideas from or "lift" onto your own cards and tags. Design tips, creative ideas, techniques and step-by-step processes have been included to assist in improving your card making skills.

Added features are our template and vellum sentiment sections. The templates can be copied or traced to make cards, tags, envelopes and boxes, and for those of us who are truly at a "loss for words" our quotes can be copied or snipped out for use right on your cards!

So, from all of us at NanC and Company to all of you who enjoy expressing yourself through handmade cards and tags – ENJOY!

Nancy

Table of Contents

Expressions of Friendship

A True Friend

Designer: Bea Elizalde

SUPPLIES Cardstock: DCWV • Patterned Paper: The Paper Co., Memories in the Making • Stickers: NRN Designs •

Eyelets: Making Memories

Beyond Basics

Create a matching envelope to go with your card. This shows the recipient you have taken extra time to make the note thoughtful.

Bamboo Card
Designer: Brenda Nakandakari
SUPPLIES Stamp: Hero Arts
• Adhesive: Hermafix

Asian Gift Bag
NanC and Campany Design
SUPPLIES Cardstock:
DCWV • Ribbon: Offray
& Son, Inc. • Charm:
Memories in the Making

Tried & True Technique

CREATE A MINI BOOKLET

1. Cut a thin piece of cardboard into a rectangle (7 1/8 x 3 1/4 inches).
2. Fold the cardboard in half.
3. Cut a patterned piece of paper 1 inch longer and 1 inch wider than the cardboard.
4. Place the patterned paper right side down on a table.
5. Apply adhesive to the wrong side of the patterned paper.
6. Center the rectangular piece of cardboard onto the patterned paper with the point of the fold facing down.
7. Smooth the paper onto the cardboard.
8. Fold the excess paper to the inside, miter the corners, and adhere.
9. Cut a sheet of cardstock into three rectangles (6 1/4 x 2 7/8 inches).
10. Fold the rectangles in half.
11. Adhere the first half of the first cardstock rectangle to the inside of the front cover with the point of the fold facing down.
12. Adhere the second half of the first rectangle to the first half of the second rectangle with both points of the folds facing down.
13. Continue adhering the pages together in this manner.
14. Finish by adhering the wrong side of the second half of the last rectangle to the inside back cover of the booklet.

Change the dimensions of the booklet to meet your needs. You can also add more pages by cutting more rectangles of cardstock.

Asian Booklet
Designer: Brenda Nakandakari
SUPPLIES Mini Scrapbook: Pixie
Press • Stamp: Stampin' Up •
Ink Pad: Colorbok

2

Expressions of Friendship

FOREVER

Friendship
makes
the sun
shine
brighter.

FRIENDS

Template on page 58

FOREVER

Forever Friends

Template Design: Phyllis Ducote
NanC and Company Design
SUPPLIES   Cardstock: DCWV •
Vellum Quote: DCWV • Stickers:
Memories in the Making • Button:
Making Memories • Small Flower
Embellishment: Jolee's Boutique

FLOWERS

Flowers

NanC and Company Design
SUPPLIES A2 Card: DCWV • Metal Letters:
Making Memories • Felt Embellishments:
Jolee's Boutique

Best Friends

Designer: Camille Jensen

SUPPLIES   Cardstock: Bazzill • Watermark
Pad: Versamark by Tsukineko • Brads: Lasting
Impressions for Paper • Embellishment:
Carolee's Creations

Friends are a Gift from God

Designer: Brindy Adams

SUPPLIES   Cardstock: DCWV, Bazzill • Patterned
Paper: Memories in the Making • Vellum: DCWV •
Stamp: Stampin' Up • Ink Pad: Stampin' Up

Friends

Designer: Bea Elizalde

SUPPLIES   Patterned Paper: Creative Memories •
Die Cuts: Sizzix • Button: Making Memories •
Metallic Accents: DCWV

Keeping in Touch

I Miss You

Designer: Miranda Isenberg

SUPPLIES   Card Template: Deluxe Cuts
• Cardstock: Creative Imaginations •
Scrabble Tiles: Making Memories •
Eyelet Letter: Making Memories • Heart
Embellishments: Sarah Heidt Photo Craft
• Button: Dress It Up! • True Love Cut
Out: SEI • Charms: Embellish It!

Just Bee Yourself

Designer: Bea Elizalde
SUPPLIES Cardstock: DCWV
• Patterned Paper: DCWV,
Frances Meyer, Inc. • Bee
Stamps: Great Impressions,
Rubber Stamps, Inc., Rubber
Stampede, Stampabilities •
Font: Jenn Penn

Beyond Basics

Make a tag to match your card.
This is a great way to enhance a
simply wrapped gift.

Bee Tag

Designer: Bea Elizalde
SUPPLIES Cardstock: DCWV
• Patterned Paper: Frances
Meyer, Inc. • Stamp: Rubber
Stampede

Flower Card

Designer: Susan Stringfellow
SUPPLIES Patterned Paper: Memories
in the Making • Ink Pad: Stampin'
Up • Adhesive: Judikins • Flower
Embellishment: ScrapYard 329

Keeping in Touch

If I had a rose for every time I thought of you, I'd walk through a garden forever.

Autumn Wreath
Designer: Bea Elizalde
SUPPLIES Cardstock: DCWV • Stamp: Anna Griffin

Miss Camille
Designer: Bea Elizalde
SUPPLIES A2 Card: DCWV • Sticker: Colorbok • Border Punch: Fiskars

Delight in Beauty
Designer: Phyllis Ducote
SUPPLIES Paper: The Crafter's Workshop • Title: Magic Scraps • Fiber: Ties That Bind • Buttons: SEI • Punch: EK Success

CREATE A POTPOURRI CARD AND TAG

1. Cut out a window in a card or tag for the potpourri to show through the card.

2. Trace and cut the same window out of a second card or tag.

3. Cut a sheer ribbon or fabric to just over double the size of the window.

4. Fold fabric in half and sew two sides to create a pocket.

5. Fill the pocket with flowers, potpourri, seeds or whatever you can imagine.

6. Sew the top closed.

7. Sew, hand stitch, tape or adhere the potpourri pocket to the backside of the window.

8. Adhere the second card or tag to cover your handiwork. If the card is too bulky, cut off the back half of the first card. For variation, cut an oval, rectangular or circular window, or cut multiple small windows. You can also stitch a pocket of potpourri to the front of a card without the window.

Flower Potpourri

NanC and Campany Design

SUPPLIES   A2 Card: DCWV •
Floss: Making Memories • Pressed
Flowers: Nature's Pressed

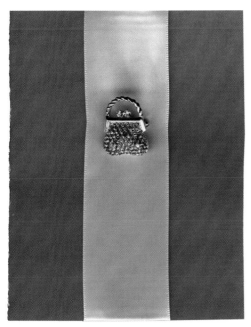

Purse

NanC and Company Design

SUPPLIES   Double
Dipped Cardstock:
DCWV • Ribbon:
Offray & Son, Inc.
• Purse   Charm:
Austrian Crystal

Thinking of You

Designer: Susan Stringfellow

SUPPLIES   Patterned Paper:
Karen Foster Design, NRN
Designs • Stamps: Stampin'
Up • Ink Pad: Versamark by
Tsukineko • Mesh: Magic Mesh
• Chalks: Craf-T Products
• Wire: Artistic Wire Ltd. •
Brad: Making Memories

Memorable Moments

Flowers

Designer: Bea Elizalde

SUPPLIES Flower Stamps: Hero Arts Rubber Stamps, Inc. • Dot Stamps: Stamps by Judith

Way to Go

Designer: Brindy Adams

SUPPLIES Cardstock: DCWV • Patterned Paper: Memories in the Making • Stamps: Stampin' Up • Ink Pad: Stampin' Up • Floss: Making Memories

Design Tip

Color a stamp with different color inkpads. Stamp a second time (without re-inking) just to the side of the original stamp to create a shadow.

Lantern

Designer: Camille Jensen
SUPPLIES   Mulberry Paper:
DCWV • Patterned Paper:
Memories in the Making •
Ink Pad: Stampa Rosa

Tried & True
Technique

WATER COLORING

Embellish your card with watercolors for a
unique look that is simple to create. Just stamp
with a watercolor stamp pad onto watercolor
paper and watercolor.

Sandals

NanC and Campany Design
SUPPLIES   A2 Card: DCWV • Floss: Making Memories • Sandal
Embellishments: Marcel Schurman Collection

Dare to Dream

Designer: Krista Fernandez
SUPPLIES   Cardstock: Paper Adventures • Patterned
Paper: Making Memories • Tag Template: Deluxe Cuts
• Slide Mount: ScrapWorks 329 • Star Embellishments:
Making Memories, Emagination Crafts Inc. • Letters: 7
Gypsies • Eyelets: Making Memories • Ribbon: Offray
& Son, Inc. • Font: Doodle Cursive

Design Tip

Use pop dots to make the
letters in the middle of the
slide mount the same height
as the letters attached to the
slide mount.

10

Terms of Endearment

with all my heart...

With All My Heart
Designer: Bea Elizalde
SUPPLIES Double Sided Cardstock: Making
Memories • Rub-ons: Making Memories •
Floss: Making Memories

*You Hold the
Key to My Heart*

Designer: Miranda Isenberg
SUPPLIES Tag: SEI • Scrabble Tiles:
Making Memories • Eyelet Letters:
Making Memories • Sticker: SEI
• Dog Tag: Clare Ultimo Inc. •
Charm: Embellish It!

Love
the more you give away, the more you have.

Believe

Designer: Tonia Borrosch
SUPPLIES Patterned Paper: Provo Craft, Daisy
D's Paper Co. • Definition: Making Memories
• Heart Vellum Tag: Making Memories • Ink:
Making Memories Love Circle Embellishment:
Keeping Memories Alive

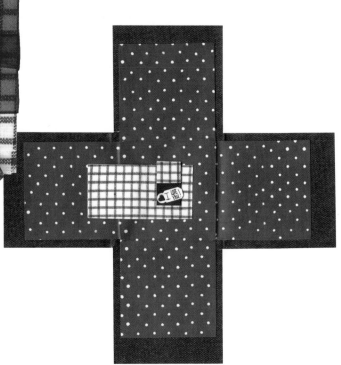

Bryan

Designer: Camille Jensen

SUPPLIES Patterned Paper: Memories in the Making • Letters: Memories in the Making

I Love You

Designer: Krista Fernandez

SUPPLIES Patterned Paper: Making Memories • Punches: EK Success • Pen: ZIG by EK Success • Metal Rimmed Tag: Making Memories • Heart Shaped Clip: Making Memories • Ribbon: Offray & Son, Inc.

13

Love, Love, Love

Designer: Susan Stringfellow

SUPPLIES   Tag Template: Deluxe Cuts • Rubber Stamp: All Night Media • Key Rubber Stamp: Stampabilities • Heart Rubber Stamp: Stampin' Up • Ink: Stampin' Up • Fibers: Fibers by the Yard • Gold Cord: Westrim Crafts • Gold Beads: Westrim Crafts • Glass Beads: All The Extras • Fonts: Black Jack Regular, Scriptina, Spring, Pegsanna, Mariah Regular, Ancient

I Love You . . .

Designer: Brindy Adams

SUPPLIES   Cardstock: DCWV • Patterned Paper: Memories in the Making • Mulberry Paper: DCWV • Stamps: Stampin' Up • Ink Pad: Stampin' Up

14

You're Invited

Baby Shower

Designer: Brande Juber

SUPPLIES A2 Card: DCWV • Cardstock: DCWV • Patterned Paper: Memories in the Making

Tried & True Technique

CREATE A TORN AND CURLED WINDOW

1. Tear the opening in the paper smaller than the finished size of the window to allow for curling.
2. Snip the corners to the finished size with scissors.
3. Curl the edges by dampening the paper with water and curling back with your fingers.
4. When the paper dries the curl will remain.

House Warming

Designer: Camille Jensen

SUPPLIES   Cardstock: DCWV •
Patterned Paper: Memories in the
Making • Stamp: Magenta Rubber
Stamps • Key Chain: Memories in
the Making • Floss: DMC • Font:
CK Sloppy

You're Invited

Designer: Camille Jensen

SUPPLIES   Patterned Paper: Memories in the Making • Metal Tags: DCWV
• Round Metal Tag: Making Memories • Metal Stamps: Foofala • Brads:
All My Memories • Eyelets: Making Memories • Floss: DMC • Paper Tags:
Memories in the Making • Stickers: Memories in the Making

Design Tip

If you are nervous about ruining a card by
making a mistake with your handwriting,
use a transparency. You can practice your
handwriting until you get it right or you
can use a computer font and print onto a
transparency. The transparency will fade
away into the background of the card.

All Aboard . . .

NanC and Company Design

SUPPLIES   A2 Card: DCWV •
Ribbon: Making Memories

Put Some Meat on Those Bones

Designer: Eleanor Howse
SUPPLIES Cardstock: DCWV •
Stickers: Frances Meyer, Inc. •
Die Cut: Deluxe Cuts

Beyond Basics

A fun die cut can make an invitation a snap to create.

This time of year we give in to the fright
Of darkness and things that go bump in the night.
The ghouls and ghosts and goblins come out.
They sneak up behind us, then "BOO" they shout.

Let's gather together, so safe we will be
Come eat, drink, be merry with Jim and me.
A costume—required—will add to the fun
Be it fireman, vampire, clown, or nun.

Maybe a witch with a tall, pointed hat;
A gypsy, a cowboy, or scary black cat.
Whatever you look like, it's sure to be great.
Just give us a call and make it a date.

Join us for
HALLOWEEN
Dinner

Saturday,
Oct. 27, 2001
7:30 P.M.

327 Westcrest St.
Jim and Eleanor
Howse

RSVP by Oct. 20th

Shhhhhh . . .
Designer: Camille Jensen
SUPPLIES   Patterned Paper: Memories in
the Making • Stamp: PSX Design • Frame:
DCWV • Star: DCWV • Oil Pastels: Crayola
• Circle Tags: Making Memories • Paper
Wire: DMD Industries

Tried & True Technique

HOW TO USE CRYSTAL LACQUER

1. Squeeze crystal lacquer onto the area
   to be highlighted.
2. Let sit for three hours to dry.

Day at the Park
Designer: Miranda Isenberg
SUPPLIES   Border Sticker: Memories in
the Making • Brads: Making Memories

Mums the Word
Designer: Maridawn Mayer
SUPPLIES   Letters: EK
Success • Circle Tags: EK
Success

Angel

NanC and Company Design

SUPPLIES Thread: Sulky
of America • Pocket Angel:
Vilmaine

Wreath

NanC and Company Design

SUPPLIES A2 Card: DCWV • Stamp:
Provo Craft • Embossing Pad: Tsukineko
• Embossing Powder: Ranger Industries •
Ribbon: Offray & Son, Inc.

Designer: Jenny Sanders
SUPPLIES Cardstock: Walmart
• Patterned Paper: Treehouse
Designs, Inc.

Love Bag

NanC and Company Design
SUPPLIES Page Pebbles:
Making Memories

Beyond Basics

Try folding a card differently so the opening is in the middle of the front of the card.

Tried & True Technique

HEAT EMBOSSING

1. Press a rubber stamp onto an embossing stamp pad.
2. Press the stamp onto the paper you wish to emboss.
3. Cover the stamped area of the paper with embossing powder.
4. Shake off the excess powder.
5. With an embossing gun heat the embossing powder on the paper until the consistency changes from a powder to a smooth finish.

Use an embossing pen to write letters or draw your own pictures to be heat embossed.

Silver Pattern

NanC and Company Design
SUPPLIES   A2 Card: DCWV •
Stamp: Stampendous! • Embossing
Pad: Tsukineko • Embossing Powder:
Ranger Industries

20

Cards of Gratitude

Thank You

Designer: Bea Elizalde

SUPPLIES   Card: The Paper Co. •
Cardstock: DCWV • Patterned Paper:
DCWV • Brads: Making Memories •
Stamp: Hero Arts • Flower Punch: Marvy
Uchida • Small Flowers: EK Success

Thank You

NanC and Company Design

SUPPLIES   A2 Card: DCWV •
Beads: Bluemoon Beads

Design Tip

Beads are a wonderful embellishment
for cards and tags. They can be sewn
on with a needle and thread or, for a
faster result, glued on.

Thanks

Designer: Maridawn Mayer
SUPPLIES Patterned Paper: DCWV •
Page Pebble Letters: Making Memories

Thank You

NanC and Company Design
SUPPLIES A2 Card: DCWV •
Papers: DCWV, Memories in the
Making • Metal Letters: DCWV

Thanks

NanC and Company Design
SUPPLIES A2 Card: DCWV • Wire Letters:
Making Memories • Ribbon Charm:
Making Memories

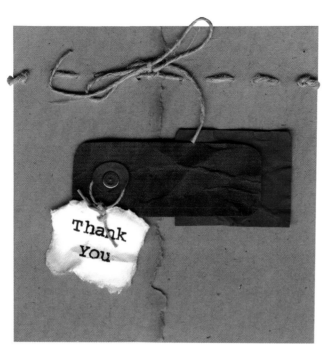

Thank You

Designer: Brindy Adams

SUPPLIES Brad: Making Memories • Button:
Making Memories • Chalk: Stampin' Up

Thank You

Designer: Camille Jensen

SUPPLIES Cardstock: DCWV • Patterned Paper:
DCWV • Metal Letters: DCWV • Metal Words:
DCWV • Brads: Lasting Impressions for Paper •
Charm Embellishments: Making Memories

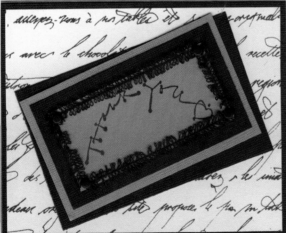

Beyond Basics

Create pockets for tags to
fit into on your card. The
receiver can pull out the tags
to read individual messages.

Thank You

Designer: Maridawn Mayer

SUPPLIES Patterned Paper: DCWV • Stamp:
Stampin' Up • Fiber: Ties That Bind

Thanks

Designer: Amanda Goodwin
SUPPLIES Cardstock: Keeping
Memories Alive • Pens: EK
Success • Embossing Powder:
UTEE by Ranger • Butterfly
Sticker: Colorbok

Thank You Tag

Designer: Bea Elizalde
SUPPLIES Patterned Paper: The Paper Co. •
Stamp: Hero Arts • Flower Punch: Marvy Uchida
• Buttons: Making Memories • Brads: Making
Memories • Wire: Making Memories

Tried & True Technique

ACCENT A STICKER WITH ULTRA THICK EMBOSSING ENAMEL (UTEE)

1. Affix a sticker to cardstock and trim around the sticker.
2. Rub the right side of the sticker on an embossing pad.
3. Cover with UTEE and shake off the excess powder.
4. With an embossing gun heat the UTEE until the consistency changes from a powder to a smooth, shiny finish.
5. Repeat steps two through four until the sticker shines to your liking.

Alter embellishments, accent words, or just add shine to your pages with UTEE.

Mini Thank You

Designer: Camille Jensen
SUPPLIES Patterned Paper: Memories
in the Making • Page Pebble: Making
Memories • Font: CK Sloppy

Thanks

Designer: Sheila Hansen
SUPPLIES A2 Card: DCWV
• Patterned Paper: Memories
in the Making • Button
Stickers: Memories in the
Making • Alphabet Stickers:
Provo Craft • Denim Pocket
Die Cut: Memories in the
Making • Tags: Pebbles in
my Pocket

New Arrival

Baa

NanC and Company Design
SUPPLIES A2 Card: DCWV •
Thread: Making Memories

Tried & True Technique

HOW TO STITCH LETTERS

1. Print or handwrite letters the same size as you would like to stitch on a piece of paper.
2. Temporarily adhere the paper to your card or tag over the area to be stitched.
3. With a needle punch holes along the letters.
4. Remove the paper after all the holes have been punched.
5. Back stitch along the holes.

You can stitch designs in the same fashion as the letters. If you would like to add beads or other embellishments to the stitches, just thread a bead on the needle when the needle is positioned at the front side of the card.

It's a Boy

Designer: Bea Elizalde
SUPPLIES   Card: The Paper Co. • Metallic
Letters: DCWV • Rub-ons: Making Memories •
Brads: Making Memories

B is for Boy

Designer: Maureen Spell
SUPPLIES Cardstock: Bazzill • Patterned Paper:
SEI • Die Cuts: Quickutz • Buttons: Dress It
Up! • Pen: ZIG by EK Success • Fibers: Fibers
by the Yard • Ink: All Night Media • Eyelet:
Making Memories

Tried & True Technique

INKING

Ink gives a weathered look to a card or just takes
away that brand new feel. To ink a card, tag or
embellishment gently rub the edges and center
with an ink pad.

Of all nature's gifts
to the human race,
what is sweeter to a man
than his **children**?

Blue

NanC and Company Design
SUPPLIES A2 Card: DCWV • Ribbon:
Offray & Son, Inc.

Happy New Baby
Designer: Camille Jensen
SUPPLIES Paper: Memories
in the Making • Metal Frame:
DCWV • Flower: Dress It Up!

Mini Happy New Baby
Designer: Camille Jensen
SUPPLIES Paper: Memories
in the Making

Beyond Basics

Create mini cards and tags from
your scraps. They are fun to give
and receive.

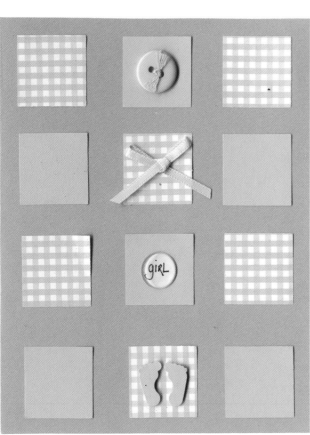

Sugar & Spice
Designer: Susan Stringfellow
SUPPLIES Cardstock: Bazzill • Tag Template:
Deluxe Cuts • Ink: Stampin' Up • Thread: Coats
& Clark • Fibers: Fibers by the Yard • Ribbon
Pinwheel: Offray & Son, Inc. • Flower: Dress It
Up! • Embossed Vellum: K & Company • Charms:
Westrim Crafts • Glass Beads: All The Extras • Brad:
Magic Scraps • Diamond Glaze Adhesive: Judikins •
Font: Scriptina

Girl
Designer: Melissa Deakin
SUPPLIES Patterned Paper: Making
Memories • Page Pebble: Making
Memories • Punch: Marvy Uchida
• Button: Dress It Up! • Ribbon:
Offray & Son, Inc.

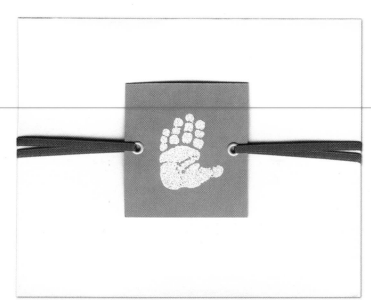

Handprint

NanC and Company Design

SUPPLIES A2 Card: DCWV • Cardstock: DCWV • Stamp: Inkadinkado • Embossing Pad: Tsukineko • Embossing Powder: Ranger Industries • Eyelets: Making Memories • Ribbon: Offray & Son, Inc. • Tag – Floss: Two Busy Moms • Metal Embellishment: Memories in the Making

Beyond Basics

Crimp paper, cardstock or embellishments to add texture and interest to your cards and tags. To crimp, simply run paper through a crimping machine.

Lincoln

Lion

NanC and Company Design

SUPPLIES A2 Card: DCWV • Cardstock: DCWV • Label: DCWV • Wire Accent: Pier 1 Imports

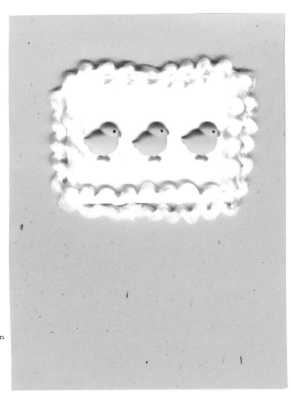

Ducks

NanC and Company Design

SUPPLIES A2 Card: DCWV • Cardstock: DCWV

Mother's Day

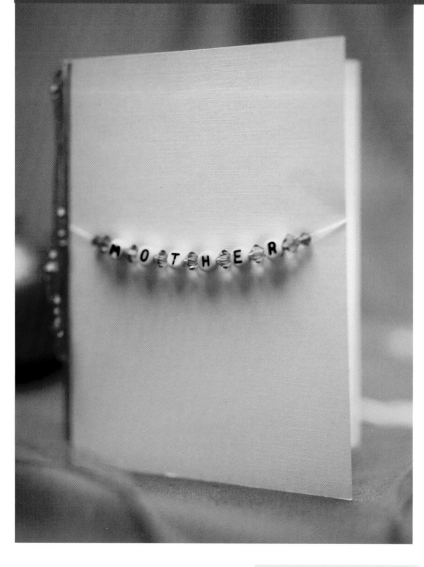

Mother

NanC and Company Design
SUPPLIES A2 Card:
DCWV • Thread:
Making Memories

Tried & True
Technique

CREATE TASSELS WITH BEADS AND FLOSS

1. Wrap embroidery floss around a card or tag.

2. Separate the strands of the floss to make more tassels.

3. With a needle, thread the beads onto the floss.

4. To secure the beads, loop the floss through the last bead and tie a knot.

5. Have the beads fall to different heights and trim off the excess floss.

Mothers

Designer: Camille Jensen

SUPPLIES Cardstock: DCWV
• Patterned Paper: Memories
in the Making • Page Pebble:
Making Memories • Button:
Making Memories • Ribbon:
Offray & Son, Inc.

God could not be
everywhere and therefore
He made mothers.
–Jewish proverb

MOTHER.

Mother

NanC and Company Design

SUPPLIES A2 Card: DCWV • Metallic
Frames: DCWV • Buttons: Making
Memories • Ribbon: Offray & Son, Inc.

Beyond Basics

Embellish a card with coordinating tags.

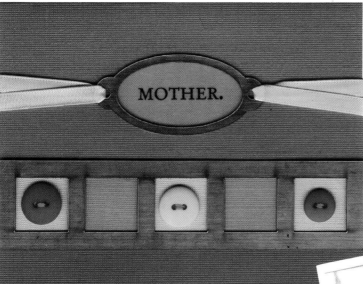

#1 mom

#1 Mom

Designer: Ashley Smith

SUPPLIES A2 Card: DCWV • Tag:
DCWV • Beads: Me & My Big Ideas

Father's Day

Dad Gift and Card

NanC and Company Design

SUPPLIES Cardstock: DCWV • Ribbon
Offray & Son, Inc.

Tried & True
Technique

CONVERTING COLOR PHOTOS TO BLACK AND WHITE OR SEPIA

1. If the photo is not digital, scan it.
2. Open the photo in a photo manipulation software program.
3. Change the image from color to black and white or sepia.

4. Save the new image.
5. Print the image.

This is a useful technique if a black and white photo will compliment the theme of your card or tag.

THERE IS NO MORE
LOVELY, FRIENDLY,
AND CHARMING
RELATIONSHIP,
COMMUNION,
OR COMPANY THAN
A GOOD MARRIAGE.

—Martin Luther

A new baby
is like the
beginning
of all things:
wonder, hope,
and a dream of
possibilities.

FEAR LESS, HOPE MORE.

WHINE LESS, BREATHE MORE.

TALK LESS, SAY MORE.

HATE LESS, LOVE MORE.

AND ALL GOOD THINGS

ARE YOURS.

—SWEDISH PROVERB

LOVE
IS BORN OF FAITH,
LIVES ON HOPE,
AND DIES OF CHARITY.

—UNKNOWN

FRIENDSHIP

Friendship isn't a big thing - it's a million little things.

Some people come
into our lives,
leave footprints
in our hearts,
and we are never
ever the same.

MY
HEART
IS
EVER AT
YOUR
SERVICE.

—Shakespeare

Happy Marriage
is a
Long Conversation
which always
seems too short.

—ANDRE MAUROIS

FEAR LESS, HOPE MORE;

WHINE LESS, BREATHE MORE;

TALK LESS, SAY MORE;

HATE LESS, LOVE MORE;

AND ALL GOOD THINGS

ARE YOURS.

—SWEDISH PROVERB

A new baby

is like the

beginning

of all things:

wonder, hope,

and a dream of

possibilities.

THERE IS NO MORE

LOVELY, FRIENDLY,

AND CHARMING

RELATIONSHIP,

COMMUNION,

OR COMPANY THAN

A GOOD MARRIAGE.

—Martin Luther

LOVE
IS BORN OF FAITH,
LIVES ON HOPE,
AND DIES OF CHARITY.
—UNKNOWN

FRIENDSHIP
Friendship isn't a big thing - it's a million little things.

A
Happy Marriage
is a
Long Conversation
which always
Seems too short.

—ANDRÉ MAUROIS

MY
HEART
IS
EVER AT
YOUR
SERVICE.

—Shakespeare

Some people come

into our lives,

leave footprints

in our hearts,

and we are never

ever the same.

baby

a new hand to hold
new heart to love
new life to lead

The
Highest Happiness on Earth
is in Marriage.

—WILLIAM LYON PHELPS

they say that **age** is all in your mind.

the **trick** is keeping it from creeping down

into your **body.**

thanks
for the
memories

take
pride

in how far
you've come,

have
faith

in how far
you can go.

I
love thee,
I love but thee
With a love
that shall not die
Till the sun grows cold
And the stars grow old...

...

—BAYARD TAYLOR

I WOULD
MAINTAIN THAT
THANKS ARE THE
HIGHEST FORM
OF THOUGHT;
AND THAT
GRATITUDE IS
HAPPINESS
DOUBLED BY
WONDER.

- G.K. CHESTERTON

Today you can be anything you

imagine

a new hand to hold
new heart to love
new life to lead

Highest Happiness on Earth

—WILLIAM LYON PHELPS

& for the
memories

they say that **age** is all in your mind,
the **trick** is keeping it from creeping down
in how far
you've come,

**have
faith**
in how far
you can go.

I WOULD
MAINTAIN THAT
THANKS ARE THE
HIGHEST FORM
OF THOUGHT;
AND THAT
GRATITUDE IS
HAPPINESS
DOUBLED BY
WONDER.

—G.K. CHESTERTON

May you can be anything you

imagine

RLB

NanC and Company Design

SUPPLIES A2 Card: DCWV • Metal
Letters: Making Memories

Design Tip

Don't throw away your scraps! They can be paper pieced to create wonderful cards and tags.

Happy Fathers Day

Designer: Camille Jensen

SUPPLIES A2 Card: DCWV • Cardstock: DCWV • Patterned
Paper: Memories in the Making • Letter Stickers: Memories
in the Making • Brads: Lasting Impressions for Paper •
Circle Tag: Making Memories

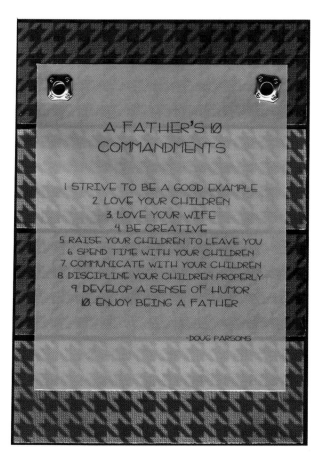

A FATHER'S 10
COMMANDMENTS

1 STRIVE TO BE A GOOD EXAMPLE
2. LOVE YOUR CHILDREN
3. LOVE YOUR WIFE
4. BE CREATIVE
5. RAISE YOUR CHILDREN TO LEAVE YOU
6. SPEND TIME WITH YOUR CHILDREN
7. COMMUNICATE WITH YOUR CHILDREN
8. DISCIPLINE YOUR CHILDREN PROPERLY
9. DEVELOP A SENSE OF HUMOR
10. ENJOY BEING A FATHER

-DOUG PARSONS

A Father's 10 Commandments

Designer: Miranda Isenberg

SUPPLIES Patterned Paper: Memories in
the Making • Eyelets: Making Memories •
Font: Two Peas in a Bucket Architect

Valentine's Day

2004

NanC and Company Design

SUPPLIES Cardstock: DCWV • Patterned Paper:
Memories in the Making • Vellum Quote:
DCWV • Metal Letters: Making Memories

Bee Mine

Designer: Miranda Isenberg

SUPPLIES Letter Stickers: Creative
Imaginations • Diecut: Quickutz

Button Heart

NanC and Company Design

SUPPLIES Cardstock: DCWV • Buttons:
ScrapArts • Thread: Two Busy Moms

Tried & True Technique

MACHINE STITCHING

1. Make sure your machine is
   properly threaded.
2. Always practice on a scrap piece
   of paper of the same thickness
   you will be stitching on for your
   card or tag.
3. Adjust the tension or needle as
   necessary.
4. It may be helpful to temporarily
   adhere what you will be stitching
   so there won't be any movement
   as you stitch.
5. Stitch your card or tag.

Easter Egg

NanC and Company Design

SUPPLIES   Cardstock: DCWV •
Wire: Making Memories

Design Tip

Use different fabrics and materials when
making cards and tags. The textures
add interest to the card or tag. Many
different materials can be used: felt, velvet,
corduroy, linen, satin and cheesecloth.

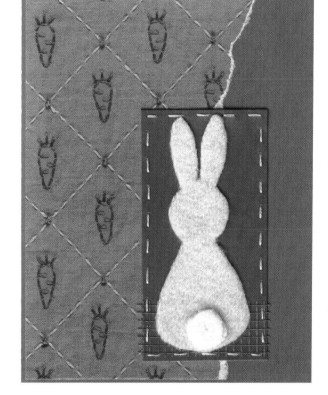

Bunny

Designer: Susan Stringfellow

SUPPLIES   Patterned Paper: Daisy D's Paper Co. • Velveteen Fabric:
Hancock Fabrics • Floss: DMC • Mesh: Magic Mesh

Easter Tag

NanC and Company Design

SUPPLIES Tag: DCWV • Wire: Making
Memories • Metal Embellishment:
Making Memories • Button: Making
Memories • Thread: Making Memories
• Ribbon: Offray & Son, Inc.

Fourth of July

Red, White and Blue

NanC and Company Design

SUPPLIES   A2 Card: DCWV •
Cardstock: DCWV • Star Buttons:
Making Memories

Freedom Tag

NanC and Company Design

SUPPLIES   Tag: DCWV •
Buttons: Making Memories •
Floss: Making Memories

Tried & True Technique

THE MANY WAYS TO USE MICRO BEADS

1. Double sided tape —dip a cut piece of tape into a bag of micro beads to coat the adhesive side of the tape. Then remove the protective paper to reveal the second adhesive side. Adhere to your card or tag.

2. Glue — apply glue to the area where the micro beads will go. Sprinkle the wet glue with the micro beads. Allow the glue to dry.

3. Watch crystal — fill a watch crystal with micro beads and adhere to your card or tag.

4. Shadow box — fill a shadow box with micro beads and attach the shadow box to your card or tag.

Boo

Designer: Susan Stringfellow

SUPPLIES   Patterned Paper: Provo Craft •
Embossing Powder: Stamps 'n' Stuff • Circle
Clip: Making Memories • Stickers: Bo-Bunny
Press, All The Extras • Fibers: Fibers by the
Yard • Eyelet: BagWorks Inc. • Foam Tape:
Magic Mounts

Pumpkins

NanC and Company Design

SUPPLIES   Cardstock: DCWV, Bazzill • Metal
Word: DCWV • Floss: All My Memories, Daisy
D's Paper Co. • Eyelet: Making Memories

Happy Halloween

Designer: Brenda Nakandakari

SUPPLIES   Tag Template: Deluxe Cuts •
Adhesive: Hermafix • Bat: Sizzix • Chalk:
Craf-T Products • Font: Horror

powder to a smooth finish.

Tried & True
Technique

CREATE A MOSAIC LOOK WITH
PATTERNED PAPER AND EMBOSSING POWDER

1. Cover a tag with two-way glue.
2. Cut patterned paper into shapes.
3. Place shapes onto glued tag, leaving space in-between each shape.

4. Sprinkle tag with embossing powder and shake off the excess powder.
5. With an embossing gun heat the embossing powder until the consistency changes from a

Enhance any embellishment or paper with embossing powder.

Thanksgiving

A Season of Change
Designer: Bea Elizalde
SUPPLIES Double Sided Cardstock: The Paper Co. • Rub-ons: Making Memories

Give Thanks
Designer: Bea Elizalde
SUPPLIES Double Sided Cardstock: The Paper Co. • Rub-ons: Making Memories • Wreath: Jolee's Boutique • Leaf Border Punch: Fiskars

Design Tip

If you don't like the look of your handwriting or would like a variety of lettering, use rub-ons as a fast and easy alternative.

Shalom

Designer: Camille Jensen

SUPPLIES   Cardstock: DCWV • Letter
Stencil: Words Worth Stamps • Snowflakes:
Provo Craft • Metal: Art Emboss • Prisma
Glitter: Close To My Heart

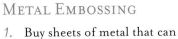

Tried & True Technique

METAL EMBOSSING

1. Buy sheets of metal that can be embossed.
2. Trace or draw your own design on the metal or place a pattern onto the sheet of metal.
3. Trace the pattern with a stylus or, for a fuller look, the eraser of a pencil.
4. Cut the pattern or design out and attach to a card or tag.

You can simply cut the metal, cut out letters, or even use your punches on the metal (if it is soft enough) for a nice embellishment to a card or tag.

Shalom Box

Designer: Camille Jensen

SUPPLIES   Brush Marker:
Tombow • Brads: Lasting
Impressions for Paper •
Metal Letters: DCWV

Template on page 59

Happy Hanukkah

Designer: Camille Jensen

SUPPLIES   Cardstock: DCWV • Patterned Paper:
DCWV • Stamp: Hero Arts • Sparkle Powder: All
Night Media • Adhesive: Xyron Machine • Gold
Vellum: DCWV • Prisma Glitter: Close To My Heart

Christmas

Christmas Joy

Designer: RoseMarie Sutton

SUPPLIES   Card: The Paper Co.
• Paper: Bo-Bunny Press, Hobby
Lobby • Stamp: Inkadinkado

Beyond Basics

Stamp a pattern onto a die cut.

Happy Holidays

Designer: Brindy Adams
SUPPLIES A2 Card: DCWV • Cardstock:
DCWV • Stamps: Stampin' Up • Ink Pad:
Stampin' Up • Floss: Making Memories

Beyond Basics

Use a border punch with double
sided cardstock to have the
second color show through to
the front of a card.

Christmas Tree Tag

Designer: Miranda Isenberg
SUPPLIES   Mosaic Tiles: Sarah
Heidt Photo Craft

Oh Christmas Tree

Designer: Bea Elizalde
SUPPLIES   Double Sided Cardstock:
The Paper Co. • Mulberry Paper:
DCWV • Border Punch: Fiskars •
Font: Script

40

Christmas

Do You See What I See?

Designer: Susan Stringfellow
SUPPLIES   Patterned Paper: Memories in the Making • Snowflake Vellum: Memories in the Making • Stamp: Close To My Heart • Eyelets: All The Extras • Mesh: Magic Mesh

Snow

Designer: Susan Stringfellow
SUPPLIES   Patterned Paper: Memories in the Making • Sticker: Memories in the Making • Punch: Marvy Uchida • Foam Tape: Magic Mounts • Wire: Artistic Wire Ltd. • Glitter: Creative Beginnings • Ribbon: Offray & Son, Inc.

Twelve Days of Christmas

Designer: Susan Stringfellow
SUPPLIES   Stamps: Stampin' Up • Ink: Stampin' Up • Fibers: Fibers by the Yard • Gold Mesh: Hancock Fabrics • Eyelets: All The Extras • Diamond Glaze Adhesive: Judikins

Beyond Basics

Making a tag for each of the twelve days of Christmas is a wonderful idea. They can be used on each page of a mini book or can be attached to a gift, especially if you are doing the twelve days of Christmas for a friend or neighbor.

How to Dry Emboss Vellum

1. Place vellum on a soft surface like a mouse pad.
2. Position a stencil under the vellum.
3. Using a stylus, trace the stencil or create your own design, being careful not to push to hard.
4. Use either side of the embossed vellum.

Try dry embossing on cardstock and other papers.

Silver Pattern
Designer: Ashley Smith
SUPPLIES A2 Card: DCWV • Cardstock: DCWV

Snowman Tag
Designer: Stacy Frandsen
SUPPLIES Snowman Template: Making Memories • Stamp: Stampin' Up • Glitter: Stampin' Up • Glue Pen: ZIG by EK Success

Merry Christmas from Our Home to Yours
Designer: Leah Fung
SUPPLIES Patterned Paper: Making Memories • Corrugated Cardboard: DMD Industries • Eyelets: Making Memories • Holly Vine Wire: Westrim Crafts • Font: CK Chemistry

Happy Holidays
Designer: Ashley Smith
SUPPLIES A2 Card: DCWV • Cardstock: DCWV • Stamps: Hero Arts • Brads: Making Memories • Charms: Jolee's Boutique

Birthday Wishes

Happy Birthday To You

Designer: Camille Jensen

SUPPLIES A2 Card: DCWV • Patterned Paper: Memories in the Making • Thread: Coats & Clark

Birthday Tags

Designer: Susan Stringfellow

SUPPLIES Patterned Paper: Memories in the Making • Letter Stickers: Memories in the Making: Mesh: Magic Mesh • Stamp: Hero Arts • Ink: Stampin' Up • Fibers: Fibers by the Yard • Foam Tape: Magic Mounts

Make a Wish

Designer: Camille Jensen

SUPPLIES Cardstock: Bazzill, DCWV • Stamp: Rubber Stampede • Eyelets: Making Memories

Design Tip

Use a variety of threads and fibers to embellish cards and tags.

Happy Birthday

Designer: Jenny Sanders

SUPPLIES Cardstock: Walmart • Glue: Mono by Tombow

Birthday Wishes

Tried & True Technique

PAPER TEARING

Tearing paper is one of the most often used techniques in card and tag making. To have more control when you tear your paper, wet the area of the paper you want to tear and tear while the paper is still wet.

Happy Birthday

Designer: Maridawn Mayer
SUPPLIES Patterned Paper: Bazzill • Stamp: Stampin' Up

Candle

Designer: Miranda Isenberg
SUPPLIES A2 Card: DCWV • Cardstock: DCWV • Patterned Paper: Paper Adventures • Candle Die Cut: Sizzix • Font: DJ Squared

Happy Boof Day

Designer: Miranda Isenberg
SUPPLIES Card Template: Deluxe Cuts • Cardstock: Creative Imaginations • Buttons: Dress It Up! • Ladybug Charm: Embellish It!

Happy Birthday, Dad

Designer: Sheila Toppi

SUPPLIES Cardstock: Bazzill • Patterned Paper: Rebecca Sower, PSX Design • Paper Frame: Provo Craft • Buttons: Dress It Up! • Stamps: PSX Design • Cork: Hygloss Products, Inc. • Ink: Brilliance by Tsukineko • Floss: DMC • Adhesive: Xyron, ZIG by EK Success

Tried & True Technique

HOW TO WALNUT INK

1. Mix walnut crystals with water according to package directions.
2. Apply walnut ink with a brush, q-tip or cotton ball.
3. Allow ink to dry.

There are other ways to accomplish an aged look: ink, crumpled paper, chalk or tea dye.

Wanted: Cool Hand Jake

Designer: Camille Jensen

SUPPLIES Patterned Paper: Karen Foster Design, Memories in the Making • Stamps: Hero Arts • Ink Pad: Staz-on by Tsukineko • Walnut Ink: 7 Gypsies • Horse Charm: Memories in the Making

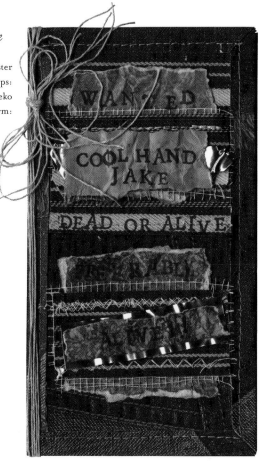

Susan

Designer: Sheila Hansen

SUPPLIES A2 Card: DCWV • Patterned Paper: Memories in the Making • Sticker: Memories in the Making

46

Health & Happiness

Herbs

NanC and Company Design

SUPPLIES A2 Card: DCWV

Bee Happy

Designer: Bea Elizalde

SUPPLIES Double Dipped Cardstock: DCWV • Alphabitties: Provo Craft • Bee Stamp: Great Impressions Rubber Stamps Inc.

Bouquet of Flowers

Designer: Bea Elizalde

SUPPLIES Cardstock: Bazzill • Punches: EK Success • Beads: Making Memories

Flower

Designer: Susan Stringfellow

SUPPLIES Patterned Paper: NRN Designs • Die Cut: NRN Designs • Stamps: Hero Arts • Border Stickers: NRN Designs • Ribbon: All The Extras • Ink: Stampin' Up • Glitter: Creative Beginnings

Beyond Basics

Use different size and style punches to create your own embellishment.

48

Flowers

Designer: Camille Jensen

SUPPLIES Cardstock: DCWV • Patterned Paper: Memories in the Making • Stamp: Magenta Rubber Stamps • Buttons: Making Memories

Smile

Designer: Susan Stringfellow

SUPPLIES Patterned Paper: Daisy D's Paper Co., Making Memories, Colorbok • Stamps: Stampin' Up • Ink: Stampin' Up • Word Stickers: Bo-Bunny Press • Fibers: Fibers by the Yard

Design Tip

Ribbons add a nice texture and the finishing touch to any card or tag.

Get Well

Designer: Tonia Borrosch
SUPPLIES Patterned Paper:
Provo Craft • Ink: Making
Memories • Definitions:
Foofala

Beyond Basics

Use a page from a
children's book to
embellish a card.

Teacup

Designer: Susan Stringfellow
SUPPLIES Patterned Paper: Making
Memories • Charms: Memories in
the Making • Punches: Creative
Memories • Thread: Coats & Clark
• Adhesive: Judikins

Got a Bug?

Designer: Brande Juber
SUPPLIES Cardstock: DCWV
• Stickers: Memories in the
Making • Eyelets: Making
Memories

Photo Greeting Cards

Wish You Were Here

NanC and Company Design

SUPPLIES Cardstock: DCWV • Patterned Paper:
Memories in the Making • Metal Letters: Making
Memories

Please join us to honor

Jennifer Payne

At a bridal shower

Saturday, May Fifteenth Two Thousand Four
At three in the afternoon

123 Main Street
Coppell

Bridal Shower

NanC and Company Design

SUPPLIES Cardstock: DCWV • Patterned
Paper: Memories in the Making • Ribbon:
Offray & Son, Inc.

The Magic of Christmas

Designer: Ashley Smith

SUPPLIES A2 Card: DCWV • Cardstock:
DCWV • Rub-ons: Making Memories

the magic of Christmas

Mother's Day

NanC and Company Design

SUPPLIES Cardstock: DCWV •
Patterned Paper: Memories in
the Making • Buttons: Making
Memories

Happy

Mother's Day

Design Tip

Photos tell what words cannot say
and are a welcome addition to
any card or tag. Personalize your
greetings with a favorite photo.

to: Grandma

McCall

Grandma Tag

NanC and Company Design

SUPPLIES Cardstock: DCWV •
Metallic Frame: DCWV

Tags

School

Designer: Leah Fung

SUPPLIES Corrugated Cardboard: DMD
Industries • Tassel: American Tag Co.
• Brads: Carolee's Creations • Wire:
Carolee's Creations • Sticker: Jolee's
Boutique • Charm: Carolee's Creations

Design Tip

Use a fabric for the
background of a tag to
add texture and interest.

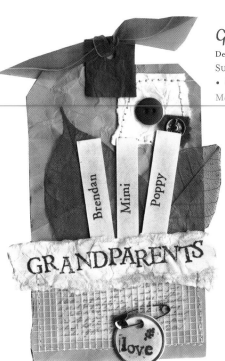

Grandparent's Love

Designer: Dee Gallimore-Perry

SUPPLIES Stamps: PSX Design, Hero Arts
• Chalk: Craf-T Products • Mesh: Magic
Mesh • Button: Hillcreek Designs

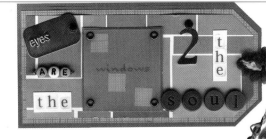

Eyes are the Windows to the Soul

Designer: Miranda Isenberg

SUPPLIES Patterned Paper: Chatterbox, Inc., SEI
• Letter Stickers: SEI • Eyelet Letters: Making
Memories • Dog Tags: Clare Ultimo Inc.

Sugar

Designer: Melissa Smith

SUPPLIES Metal: Art Emboss •
Vintage Label: Paperphernalia •
Specialty Paper: Paperphernalia

You Make My Heart Leap

Designer: Miranda Isenberg

SUPPLIES Tag Template: Deluxe Cuts • Cardstock:
Bazzill • Letter Stickers: SEI • Eyelet Letters: Making
Memories • Alphabet Nail Heads: Scrapworks,
LLC • Heart Eyelet: Creative Imaginations • Frog
Embellishment: Sarah Heidt Photo Craft

Don't Bug Me

Designer: Miranda Isenberg

SUPPLIES Tag: SEI • Scrabble
Tiles: Making Memories • Eyelet
Letters: Making Memories •
Charm: Embellish It!

Beyond Basics

Stitch pockets in tags and cards to
hold notes or special mementos.

Cowboy

Designer: Sara Horton
SUPPLIES Cardstock: Bazzill • Patterned
Paper: Karen Foster Design • Brads: Jest
Charming • Stickers: Tumblebeasts

Beyond Basics

Adhere a window on a tag or
card with pop dots to make the
contents of the window look
like they are in a shadow box.

Be Happy

Designer: Miranda Isenberg
SUPPLIES Cardstock: Bazzill • Brad:
Making Memories • Mesh: Magic
Mesh • Charm: Embellish It!

All Boy

Designer: Susan Stringfellow
SUPPLIES Patterned Paper: Memories in
the Making • Eyelets: Making Memories •
Vellum: Paper Adventures • Rope: Two Busy
Moms • Thread: Coats & Clark

Tags

To My Friend Rhonda

Designer: Melissa Smith
SUPPLIES Patterned Paper: Paper Adventures • Envelopes: Foofala • Pen: Hunt Corporation • Silver Clip: Westrim Crafts • Font: Albemarle Swash

For You

Designer: Phyllis Ducote
SUPPLIES Cardstock: Bazzill, The Crafter's Workshop • Vellum Metal Tag: Making Memories • Stickers: Mrs. Grossmans, ScrapYard 329 • Lettering: The Crafter's Workshop • Ribbon: EK Success

Beyond Basics

Create a tag booklet with vellum envelopes. Each envelope in the booklet can hold a tag with a special note or picture on it.

Swim Like a Fish

Designer: Miranda Isenberg
SUPPLIES Alphabet Nail Heads: Scrapworks, LLC

Family Travels

Designer: Martha Crowther
SUPPLIES Patterned Paper: Karen Foster Design • Tag: Rebecca Sower • Stickers: Rebecca Sower Nostalgiques • Metal Embellishments: Li'l Davis Designs • Font: Antique

Template on page 58

Copy Directions

We hope you find these templates easy and fun to use. Just copy the templates according to the following guidelines:

70% - Copy at 130%   40% - Copy at 160%

65% - Copy at 135%   20% - Copy at 180%

50% - Copy at 150%

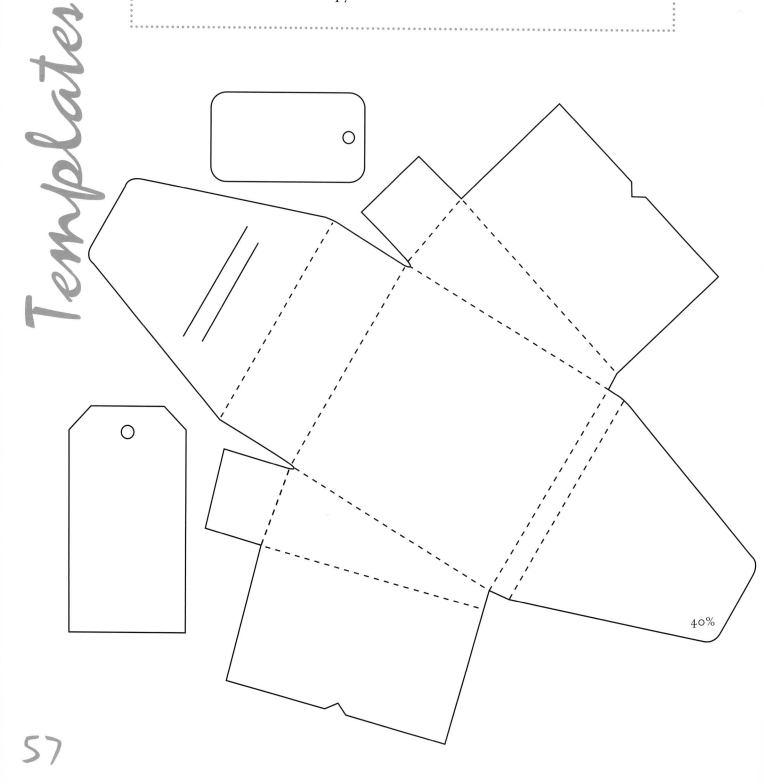

40%

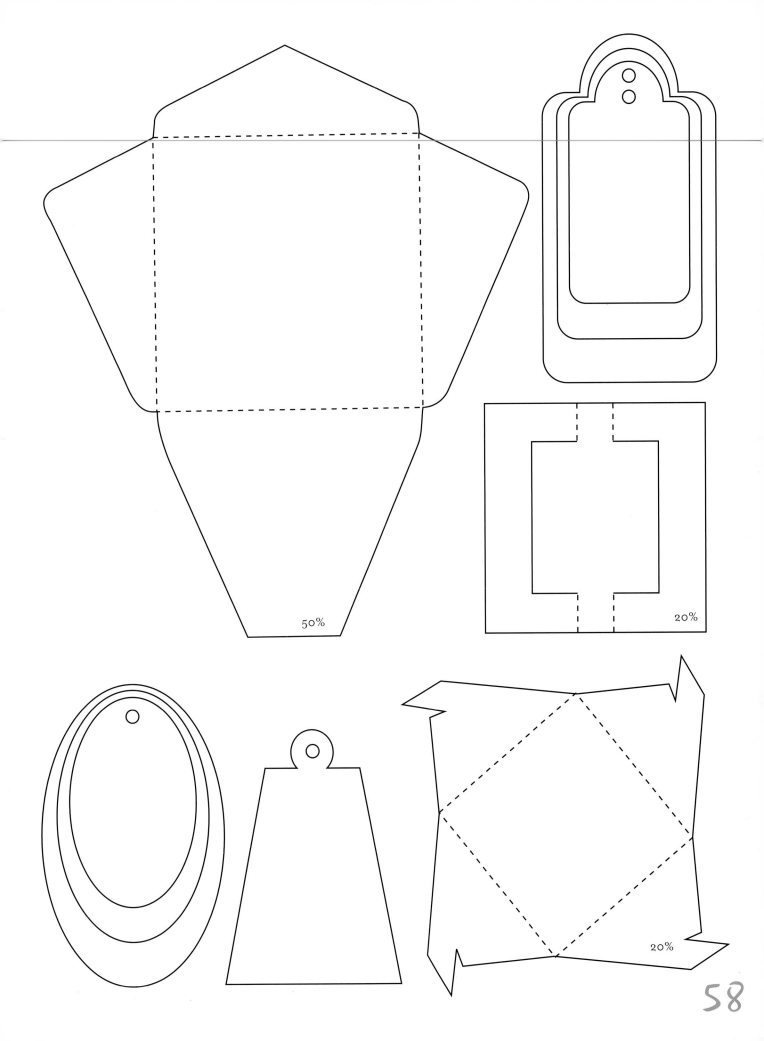

50%

20%

20%

58

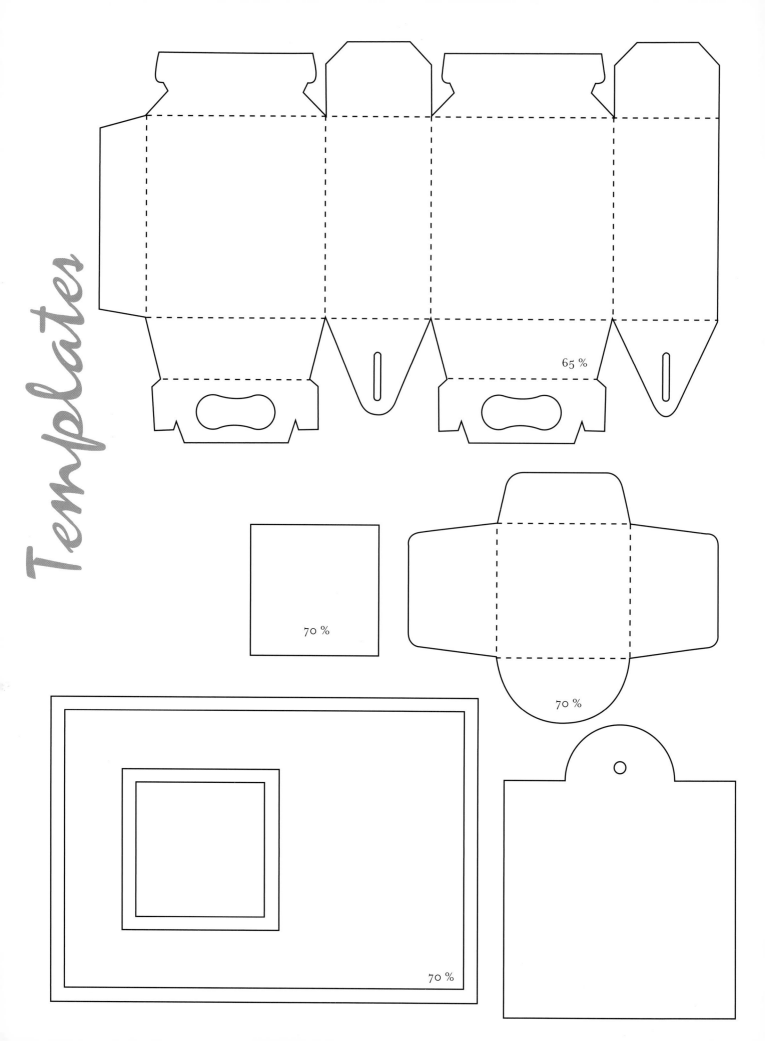

Templates

65 %

70 %

70 %

70 %

50%

70%

70%

60

Templates

70%

61

3L Corp.
(800) 828-3130
3lcorp.com

3M Stationary
(800) 364-3577
3m.com

7 Gypsies
(800) 588-6707
7gypsies.com

All My Memories
(801) 619-8838
allmymemories.com

All Night Media
(800) 842-4197
allnightmedia.com

All The Extras
alltheextras.com

American Tag Co.
(800) 642-4314
americantag.net

Anna Griffin
(888) 817-8170
annagriffin.com

Art Emboss
amaco.com

Artistic Wire Ltd.
(630) 530-7567
artisticwire.com

BagWorks Inc.
(817) 446-8105
bagworks.com

Bazzill
(480) 558-8557
bazzillbasics.com

Bluemoon Beads
(800) 377-6715
bluemoonbeads.com

Bo-Bunny Press
(801) 770-4010
bobunny.com

Carolee's Creations
(435) 563-1100
caroleescreations.com

Chatterbox, Inc.
(888) 416-6260
chatterboxinc.com

Clare Ultimo Inc.
(212) 777-6973
clareultimo.com

Close To My Heart
closetomyheart.com

Coats & Clark
coatsandclark.com

Colorbok
(800) 366-4660
colorbok.com

Craf-T Products
(800) 530-3410
craf-tproducts.com

Crafter's Workshop, The
(877) CRAFTER
thecraftersworkshop.com

Crafts Etc!
(800) 888-0321
craftsetc.com

Crayola
(800) 272-9652
crayola.com

Creative Beginnings
(800) 367-1739
creativebeginnings.com

Creative Imaginations
(800) 942-6487
cigift.com

Creative Memories
(800) 341-5275
creativememories.com

Daisy D's Paper Co.
(888) 601-8955
daisydotsanddoodles.com

DCWV
(801) 224-6766
diecutswithaview.com

Deluxe Cuts
(480) 497-9005
deluxecuts.com

DMC
(973) 589-9890
dmc-usa.com

DMD Industries
(800) 805-9890
dmdind.com

Dress It Up!
dressitup.com

EK Success
(800) 524-1349
eksuccess.com

Emagination Crafts Inc.
(866) 238-9770
emaginationcrafts.com

Embellish It!
(702) 312-1628
embellishit.com

Fibers by the Yard
fibersbytheyard.com

Fiskars
(800) 950-0203
fiskars.com

Foofala
(402) 758-0863
foofala.com

Frances Meyer, Inc.
francesmeyer.com

Great Impressions
Rubber Stamps Inc.
(360) 807-0014
greatimpressionsstamps.
com

Hancock Fabrics
(877) 322-7427
hancockfabrics.com

Herma Fix
herma.co.uk.com

Hero Arts Rubber
Stamps, Inc.
(800) 822-4376
heroarts.com

Hillcreek Designs
(619) 526-5799
hillcreekdesigns.com

Hunt Corporation
(800) 663-4868
hunt-corp.com

Hygloss Products, Inc.
(973) 458-1745
hygloss.com

Inkadinkado
(781) 938-6100
inkadinkado.com

Jest Charming
(702) 564-5101
jestcharming.com

Jolee's Boutique
joleesbyyou.com

Judikins
(310) 515-1115

K & Company
(888) 244-2083
kandcompany.com

Karen Foster Design
(801) 451-9779
karenfosterdesign.com

Keeping Memories Alive
(469) 633-9665
kimemories.com

Lasting Impressions
for Paper
(800) 936-2667

Li'l Davis Designs
(949) 838-0344
lildavisdesigns.com

Magenta Rubber Stamps
magentarubberstamps.com

Magic Mesh
(651) 345-6374
magicmesh.com

Magic Mounts
(800) 332-0050
magicmounts.com

Magic Scraps
(972) 238-1838
magicscraps.com

Making Memories
(800) 286-5263
makingmemories.com

Marcel Schurman
Collection
(707) 428-0200
shurman.com

Marvy Uchida
(800) 541-5877
uchida.com

Memories in the Making
(888) 257-7548
business.leisurearts.com

Mrs. Grossmans
(800) 429-4549
mrsgrossmans.com

Nature's Pressed
(800) 850-2499
naturespressed.com

NRN Designs
nrndesigns.com

Offray & Son, Inc.
offray.com

Paper Adventures
(800) 727-0699
paperadventures.com

Paperphernalia
(408) 736-5159
paperphernalia.com

Pixie Press
(702) 646-1156
pixiepress.com

Provo Craft
(888) 577-3545
provocraft.com

PSX Design
(800) 782-6748
psxdesign.com

Quickutz
(888) 702-1146
quickutz.com

Ranger Industries
(800) 244-2211
rangerink.com

Rebecca Sower
mississippipaperarts.com

Rubber Stampede
(800) 423-4135
rubberstampede.com

Sarah Heidt Photo Craft
(734) 424-2776
sarahheidtphotocraft.com

ScrapArts
(503) 631-4843
scraparts.com

Scrapworks, LLC
scrapworksllc.com

ScrapYard 329
(775) 829-1227
scrapyard329.com

SEI
(800) 333-3279
shopsei.com

Sizzix
sizzix.com

Stampa Rosa
stamparosa.com

Stampabilities
(800) 888-0321
stampabilities.com

Stampendous!
(800) 869-0474
stampendous.com

Stampin' Up
(800) 782-6787
stampinup.com

Stamps by Judith
stampsbyjudith.com

Stamps 'n' Stuff
stampsnstuff.com

Sulky of America
sulky.com

The Paper Co.
(800) 449-1125
papercompany.com

Ties That Bind
(505) 762-0295
tiesthatbindfiber.com

Tombow
(800) 835-3232
tombowusa.com

Treehouse Designs, Inc.
(877) 372-1109
treehouse-designs.com

Tsukineko
(800) 769-6633
tsukineko.com

Tumblebeasts
(505) 323-5554
tumblebeasts.com

Two Busy Moms
twobusymoms.com

Two Peas in a Bucket
twopeasinabucket.com

Un-Du
un-du.com

Westrim Crafts
(800) 727-2727
westrimcrafts.com

Words Worth Stamps
(719) 282-3495
wordsworthstamps.com

Xyron
(800) 793-3523
xyron.com

Upcoming Books

Look for these published or soon to be published
Leisure Arts Scrapbooking Idea Books

IT'S ALL IN YOUR IMAGINATION

IT'S ALL ABOUT BABY

IT'S ALL ABOUT SCHOOL

IT'S ALL ABOUT TECHNIQUE

IT'S ALL ABOUT PETS AND ANIMALS

IT'S ALL ABOUT TRAVEL AND VACATION

IT'S ALL ABOUT MINI ALBUMS

IT'S ALL ABOUT HERITAGE PAGES

IT'S ALL ABOUT TEENS

10-20-30 MINUTE SCRAPBOOK PAGES